LIVING IN A
TWO-FACED JUNGLE

LIVING IN A
TWO-FACED JUNGLE

Michael A. Powell

Charleston, SC
www.PalmettoPublishing.com

Living in a Two-Faced Jungle
Copyright © 2023 by Michael A. Powell

All rights reserved
No portion of this book may be reproduced, stored in a retrieval
system, or transmitted in any form by any means–electronic,
mechanical, photocopy, recording, or other–except for brief quotations
in printed reviews, without prior permission of the author.

First Edition

Hardcover ISBN: 979-8-8229-1819-1
Paperback ISBN: 979-8-8229-1820-7
eBook ISBN: 979-8-8229-1821-4

*Masks are wonderfully paradoxical in this way:
while they may hide the physical reality, they can
show us how a person wants to be seen.*

—Joanna Scott

Life is candy. Life is a game. The boys do the fucking. The girls get the blame. It is easy to push her up against the wall, pull out his reputation, stick in his education, and increase the population of the younger generation. The father is a bastard. The mother: a whore. It would not have happened if the rubber hadn't torn. Welcome to the two-faced jungle called life.

—Author unknown

TABLE OF CONTENTS

PROLOGUE
LIFE'S EQUATION

MY LIFE IS a function of my desires, multiplied by my expectations, and then divided by the choices that I make. The greater my desire, the higher my expectation, giving me a multitude of choices. However, if my desire is not that great, my expectation will not be that high, leaving me with only two choices: *bad* and *mediocre*.

—Cedric B.

LIFE ON LIFE'S TERMS
IS THE WAY WE LIVE

IF LIFE WERE a person, he would be a male. He'd be a really sharp dresser with perfect skin tone, perfect teeth, and all of that other exterior bullshit that makes you feel good and want more. But this is how the vast majority of the planet would describe him: lovable, gorgeous, fun, priceless, and beautiful. He would also be charming, breathtaking, emotional, and bipolar. Then it gets dark. This is how he will be one day. On the next day, he would be boring, tiring, unfair, two-faced, untruthful, dull, and shady as fuck. In short, life can be a smooth, calm, beautiful, two-faced, chaotic, backstabbing motherfucker that you would ever want to meet.

The birds are chirping and flying around willy-nilly and shit. They appear to be happy as fuck. The sky is so blue. Oh my God, is the sky really Carolina blue? Is Carolina blue even a bona fide color? The trees are natural, fabricated ladders that get me closer to God. How could someone ever find himself or herself running away from God instead of running toward him? I could stay in the trees forever. There is only one problem…I love climbing trees and coming back down safely without a scratch or serious injury. However, I have been getting fucked up lately. I am seriously thinking about retiring from climbing trees and shit.

There are moments—small increments of déjà vu—when I can actually smell the air of my childhood. The memories of lying in the grass, climbing trees, and jumping creeks with friends create a natural euphoria. Life was good then.

I had few worries and very little responsibility. Playing outside, passing my grade (C average), and making sure the small trashcans around the house were emptied: these were the only duties that were bestowed upon me by Mom. My one and only major worry at this point in my life was around picture-taking time. This is when my mother's boyfriend Ben would braid my hair and pick it out into an afro. Damn! That shit hurt like hell. It felt like he was pulling my damn scalp apart. The results, however, made the pain that I endured well worth it. I would have an afro for two days! My nappy ass hair stretched to the limits. Although my fucking scalp was tender and sore as hell, that mini afro with a long ass part on the side raised my self-esteem.

Welcome to my life: the two-faced jungle.

INTRODUCTION

BEFORE THE DRUGS

MANY WISE PEOPLE have said it, "Hindsight is twenty-twenty."

Therefore, a system has been established in my recovery process, which has proven to be crucial when it comes to recapitulating my life's memories in an honest and accurate story. The system starts with the memory. Realizing that some memories are real and some memories are imagined, I have concluded that there were some episodes in my life that were fabricated and retold so many times that distinguishing fact from fiction became a tedious task.

Moreover, when all of the smoke clears and the task is complete, I will have looked back on my life and sorted through the chaos and confusion. The many episodes that entail my living and life experiences are dissected and diagnosed. My memories go as far back as when I was three or four years old. I am a forty-seven-year-old Black man with vivid memories. One day while attending classes at Winston–Salem State University, I had one of those aha moments. This moment occurred while sitting in my Introduction to Psychology class. The professor was giving a lecture on the human brain. She went into a segment of the lecture that focused on the hippocampus. When she stated that the hippocampus was the catalyst for episodic memories and that it had the capability to recall exact body temperature and blood pressure when remembering episodes, I knew that I was going to be writing these memoirs after I finished graduate school.

I remember when my mother would always wake us up and get us ready to go to the babysitter's in the morning before she went to work. There was a fork in the road. If she went to the left, we would be at the good grandma's house.

And if she went to the right, then I thought, "Oh shit! Fuck!"

I did not know what abuse was back then. But, as I look back, it was definitely abuse. However, as a child with a voice inside of me, I was able to adjust to the surroundings.

This grandma and grandpa that I speak about turned out not to be kind to me at all. This is where life turns on me for the first of many times to come. I felt feelings of betrayal, anguish, hurt, confusion, guilt, and shame for the first time. I am going through this big ass, fucked up emotional roller coaster alone. In addition, nobody knows I am on it. I am at the edge of a two-faced jungle called life.

Furthermore, what is life? Is life a program? Or is it a set of situations and circumstances laced with self-will that one must maneuver through to get to the other side? On the other side is the lesson, the blessing, the course, the reward, or the trap floor. What I know so far about life is that it can and will turn on you at the drop of a dime.

At the same time, it will lift you up in euphoria to the point where you are telling yourself, "Life is good," with a dumb ass smile on your face.

In the summers, my brother, my sister, and I would have company. We found out that there were more siblings. We had fun! Those were the days! Life was good. Then one summer, I was eavesdropping. I overheard the bad grandma telling someone all my brothers and sisters were her grandkids except me. This is the point where life stopped being good for no reason. I now felt like an outcast. After further investigation, I found out that they all had the same dad. I had a different dad. Life had turned on me for the first time.

The key to keeping it real and telling the truth throughout the story is to embrace my hindsight. The formulation of insight based on hindsight leads to foresight. My foresight does not allow me to see the future. What it does allow is another look at a solution to any situation or dilemma based on what has been tried in a similar situation in the past. Therefore, my insight based on hindsight helps me develop and improve my foresight.

My first disclaimer is that I had no plausible, rational thinking when I was in the midst of the many episodes of my life. Therefore, the reader shouldn't expect any miraculous, heroic, or bullshit endings to the stories. There will, however, be an attempt to explain, compare, and contrast my then-rationale with the mindset of now. The old saying that 99.5 percent of the human population will say to themselves at least once in their lifetime—"If I only knew then what I know now…"—will become an anthem in these readings.

When all is said and done, my prayer is that the knowledge fairy will be dropping into other young souls in hopes that a connection can be made to provide encouragement, prevention, confirmation, improvement, and most of all, hope. My hope is that my story can be one of inspiration, not sadness and despair. It is my prayer that young Black boys, who inevitably reach manhood if no unforeseen problems arise, will be able to see what works and what does not. In addition, and most importantly, anticipate what is coming (foresight).

This book will recapture thoughts, activities, lessons, blessings, and episodes from my life. However close to fiction any of it may sound, I assure the reader that my sole reason for even writing these memoirs was never to deceive anyone, let alone disguise my fact-based intentions with a futile attempt to appear to be someone I am not.

BOOK ONE

CHAPTER ONE
CHILDHOOD

MY CHILDHOOD IS based on insight gained from hindsight. I am not sure how old I was in my earliest memories. I just know that I was not at any school. In addition, I experienced boredom for the first time. As I recall, this was the period in my life where I used my snooping skills to go through my grandma's shit. I would just randomly snoop around in the back of closets, under beds, and in the unused pocketbooks. I loved going through them. I was not a thief yet. I was something like a little badass private investigator. As I recall, I really was not looking for anything specific. It was all about chasing away the boredom while learning new shit. I came across some books that were very old when I was young. They would probably be worth a fortune today.

One day while on one of my snooping expeditions, I stumbled up on some new shit I was looking at a woman without clothing, and I could not stop staring. I remember this chick had my eyes locked! I could not even blink. This is the moment when my awareness of the opposite sex went to full blast. Now that I think about it, I have liked pussy since before I can remember. Wow! Although I cannot confirm this statement, I am sure that my dick got hard the moment I laid eyes on the picture. Tits and skin! I remember! Thank God for *Jet* magazine! Yeah, I remember! My dick did get hard. This life-changing experience went along with another one. I had to have been between three and four years old. My estimate is based on the address we lived at. Getting back to the story, my Mom was a social person. House parties all the damn time. I swear I know the lyrics to every top forty song of the 1970s.

There was a party. I was young, like three or four, so I was in bed when this shit went down. I am not going to even guess at the time. Let us just say it was late. I'm not sure how long it had been since I stumbled across the porn, but a woman calling my name lured me out of my slumber. What I know now is that she was being fucked really well. In addition, his name was Mike.

Mr. Mike was hitting that ass so hard that she kept on calling out, "Mike, Mike, oh Mike."

She was so convincing that she got me out of my bed in the pitch dark to see what she wanted. So, I obliged. The last thing that I remember is being up close and I startling both of them. Then I was scooted back to bed. To this very day, I have no idea who in the hell that was in our room, fucking on the floor. Nevertheless, what happened was this. A woman called out my name while wrapped in sexual bliss was forever carved into my brain. Now what the fuck does a four-year-old do with that shit?

The Two-Faced Jungle is not meant to be a fancy cliché title. It is a description of life, particularly my life. Looking back on my life, I have noticed that I had some feelings of superiority, gratitude, and self-love at the same time. During these times, life was good! Living and enjoying life is what it is about. And then, bam! Life showed me it has two faces, and I keep forgetting that the good times can be a trap. All of a sudden, I am living and feeling totally different. I am thinking that another life has possessed me until it hits me. My life has not changed. However, the situations and circumstances of my life have altered.

Therefore, just like that, life has turned on me. Shit is uncomfortable, awkward, and neurotic. I am no longer feeling happy, joyous, and free. Life has two fucking faces, which means that navigating through life without proper guidance and skills can be good and bad at the same damn time.

Please allow me to walk you through my life's lessons, blessings, mistakes, and triumphs, so that you can understand what I shared.

I can still remember all my elementary school teachers: Ms. Gunter, Ms. Campbell, Ms. Kelly, Ms. Brown, Ms. Zick, Ms. Leonard, and Mr. Fowler. Their faces are as clear to me as if it were yesterday. Unbelievably, elementary school would have a tremendous effect on my life.

The early years were good. No worries. No responsibilities equaled no problems. Hell, I did not even know that we were poor back then until I got older. The earliest memories that I have are so priceless to me. Kindergarten was fun. I could not get enough of that fucking Mr. M with the munching mouth. Moving from day care into kindergarten was a culture shock. I did, however, adjust to the structure easily. I loved going to school.

One of the things that I did notice early in all my elementary classes was that I was never placed with my neighborhood friends. The school was not even that big. It was all good, though. The white kids would have to do. They played and talked differently. They even paid no mind to our physical differences. This atmosphere would last until the third grade.

In third grade, I recall being the only Black boy in the class. This did not bother me at all at first! Life was good. I was living a happy, carefree life with no stress or drama. When I think back, I had already been through two or three girlfriends by this time. That is another chapter. LOL.

Ms. Brown's third grade class was not exciting, and it was not the most popular class in the school either. The popular classes were the ones that had my neighborhood friends.

"What the hell is going on with the separation of me and my friends?"

To make things worse, Ms. Brown apparently needed help. A big, fat Black woman named Ms. Johnson was going to be our teacher's aide, and she was mean! I was thinking that I could charm her with my personality and my smile. She was not feeling any of that shit. I do not think that she even had the ability to smile.

From the time she got to my class until the end of the third-grade year, she was in my shit. Forty years later, I can see how she was an angel (the first of two) that God had sent especially for me. But understand this. She only gained angel status in my eyes based on hindsight. I hated her for years until I finally came to understand her true purpose for entering my life. My third-grade experience could have driven me to the lowest levels of self-esteem, bitterness, insanity, and depression. What happened to me was not unique, and I have the feeling that this also happened to young Black boys all over the country.

Then there was Ms. Johnson. She was the meanest, ugliest, nitpickiest person that I had ever known in my eight-and-a-half years of life. She was always fucking with me about things that I thought at the time were dumb shit. Now she is an angel? I guess I had better start explaining this one.

CHAPTER TWO

THE DISCOVERY: BLACK AND WHITE

I AM NOT sure of what day of the week it was or the time. My memory is not that precise, and I would describe it as hyperepisodic.

We were in a history reading session, and it was my turn to read. My voice was loud because I enjoyed reading. During my reading, I remember the storyline leading up to the point where the white people owned the Black people in history. This was what some smart motherfucker considered a subtle introduction to one of the greatest tragedies known to humankind: the institution of slavery. The book was talking some shit about slave masters, slave ships, and escapes. It went on to talk about whipping, sailing, buying, and trading slaves. By the end of the class reading session, it had been established that white people were superior to Black people, that slavery was just something that happened, and that there was no wrongdoing.

I remember going home confused as fuck. The school bus was rowdy and loud as usual. Why was everybody so fucking happy? Did they not just read the same shit that I read? I would later come to understand that I was the only one on the bus who had read that garbage. My reading level was high, and I was in an advanced class all the way through elementary. This is why I was never with my friends.

That next day in class was really a trip! Not only was I confused and in a daze, but the white kids seemed a little confused as well. Depending on parenting and home life, some white kids would then go on to embrace their fake ass superiority, while others would dismiss the belief totally. In addition, some appeared to be sympathetic. As for me, I was offended. The separation process was a success. That evil person who placed the history books throughout the third-grade classes in America had succeeded. Even though we had innocently played together last week, unaware of racism and separatism, we would now be divided by skin color for the rest of our lives. Now I understand how they can calculate how many prisons to build based on third- and fourth-grade test scores. The knowledge gained from that book seriously resembled Adam and Eve's experience with the apple. Nothing good came from it at all. I did not believe any of that shit! It had to be wrong or incorrect.

Now, let us look at the damage caused. Even though I absolutely did not buy into the bullshit, just think about how many Black third graders across the United States of America went home after ingesting the fake news that they were inferior, actually believing that shit. Just thinking about the numbers of individuals who were negatively affected sickens me to my stomach. I felt powerless for the first time. Despair and depression soon followed. I was in trouble.

Before this string of rude awakenings fell upon me, life was good. "Ignorance is bliss" is an old quote that I have always heard. However, I could never relate to the words. Boy, was I ignorant on so many levels. I did not know that I was poor or that racial inequalities existed. I did not even know that my brother and sister were not my full siblings. We were only half siblings. All this new information...damn. What is going on? Before the bad news, I was a little boy with little boy issues. I played with Army men. I ran through the woods and jumped creeks and shit. In addition, going to Piney Grove to get a free lunch in the summer was like going out of town. Life was good. Then, all of a sudden, bam! Life turned on me. One minute, I loved living and breathing. I loved getting up in the morning. This marked the first time that I can truly remember when life turned on me. I'm saying life turned on me on a regular basis in my early days.

Grandma said, "If you fool me once, shame on you. But if you fool me twice, shame on me."

Life gave me a curve on this episode. Nevertheless, I had not even considered stamping the two-faced label on it.

MS. JOHNSON

"Tuck your shirt in! Fix your pants! Go straight to the restroom and wash your face!"

These were some commands that I would receive first thing in the morning when I touched down at Old Richmond Elementary. I hated that shit! Now that I think back, even though Ms. Johnson was introduced to the class as a teacher's aide, Ms. Brown wasn't there. Maybe she had an illness or something. All I know is this. Ms. Johnson took over that motherfucking class. In my mind, her sole purpose was to fuck with me every day. She became an expert at it. She would lecture me every day about dumb shit.

She would always look me up and down, checking for neatness as well as cleanliness. "Hygiene, Michael."

This is what she would whisper to me every morning. She would even check my nails! She was doing shit that my Mom would do sometimes. However, my Mom would do it and say it with a loving smile or touch. Ms. Johnson, on the other hand, never smiled. I did not detect a loving or caring bone in her body. Two people telling me the same shit. My Mom's orders seemed like they were optional. I was lazy as hell. So optional was another word for "I am not doing it because I do not feel like it." Ms. Johnson made all her shit seem mandatory. It felt like that shit was the law.

As the third grade rolled on, I became a fucking neat freak. I began to want to please her. Some days I would pass the hygiene and neatness test, and some days I would fail. Then she would call me outside to give me a lecture on how to match my damn clothes. I remember thinking to myself, "This motherfucker!" It was hard to please her! Not only did I have to clean my fingernails, but I had to be neatly dressed every day. Brushing my teeth became mandatory. Combing my hair and coordinating the colors of my clothes was slowly becoming the norm. I say slowly because, naturally, I was bucking her ass.

In the beginning, I thought that Ms. Johnson was the meanest woman that I had ever met. I thought that she was singling me out. I felt picked on and humiliated every time the name "Michael Powell" was called to the hallway for a lecture or scolding. I had no way of knowing that she was a gift from heaven.

SUMMARY

The third grade would be the second episode of my life where I felt that life itself had turned against me. I mean, all that was going on with me before the betrayal was typical eight-year-old, third-grader shit. Then one day during my reading period, I find out that Black people are believed to be inferior and were previously owned by white people called slave masters. My world was crushed. All my former white friends were going to get the wrath of Mike Peezy! Not only did life just reveal to me that I belonged to an inferior race, but this big Black woman also came into my life and took it over at a dark time. Life had done it again. This was a false alarm, though. Fear, insecurity, and low self-esteem had me in a chokehold. My perception was distorted, leaning in the negative.

I get it now, but I did not get it then. If I had not been infatuated with my fantasies, I would be well on my way. I have always been in love with my fantasies. In fact, I love them so much that I maintain a constant resentment toward reality. Reality always goes against my fantasies. This dilemma continued throughout my life until I learned that it was easier to change my perception of life than life itself. But the shit that I just said may sound good on paper and in my head. But it still has an easier-said-than-done connotation.

Furthermore, I remember accepting the fact that life had double-crossed me by sending Ms. Johnson my way. I remember the day when she was packing up her stuff, but I did not want to see her leave. She saved me from a spiral that I could not have recovered from. She made me take pride in my hygiene, my attire, and my black skin. I was the only Black kid in Ms. Brown's third grade class. She gave me the attention that I needed to navigate through the psychological trauma from reading that biased historical bullshit. Most of all, I learned that perception mattered. What I saw as a curse in the beginning turned out to be a blessing from God. Although life did, in fact, show that it was two-faced, God showed his face.

CHAPTER THREE

THE GIRLS RAISED IN THE SOUTH (THE GRITS)

DAMN, I LIKE thick, buttery ass grits. Something in me makes me want to be around them. This same something makes me want to do nasty shit to them and with them when we are alone, and nobody is around. I noticed that some were willing but some were not having that shit. Keep in mind that this freaky and kinky mind has been this way since I heard another Mike sexing on my room floor late night when I was three or four years old. Even today, I can still hear her calling my name while she was in sexual bliss. Now that scene will always live in my memories for eternity. This is why I love me some pussy to this day!

That is right. I'm being very honest. I loved pussy but was terrified of it at the same damn time. I did not get any pussy until I was in high school. However, I love it so much that I knew that I would master the art of fucking. It turns out that the shit pretty much came naturally. Nevertheless, it was after the summer of my first year of high school would I bust an actual nut. However, there was a whole lot of jerking off before my virginity was gone. And I mean a lot! Shit. My hands were really my first sexual partners. The left was my favorite. However, the right hand was for special occasions.

The funny part about the whole "get pussy" campaign that was going on all those years was that when I finally got it, after it all went down, I was so disappointed. My heart was broken. Pussy was overrated. That shit was over in two or three pumps.

I do, however, remember this song playing repeatedly in my head: pussy is overrated; pussy is overrated. All those years, all the hype, and all the beating my meat until that shit was sore was a bunch of bullshit.

Pussy is powerful. Wars have started over pussy. A perfect example of the previous statement would be Helen of Troy. Now, I do not know how Miss Helen looked. But I will bet anything that the pussy was super good! This is what I have learned over the years since taking the plunge into that first piece of pussy. Women can and will use that shit as a weapon. They are aware they can get some dick anytime that they want. Choice dick! They would be offended if an undesirable cracked on the skins. They would even go home to a significant other and tell them what happened. However, let an attractive motherfucker howl at the same chick, and she is going to fuck! Especially if there is a 100 percent chance that she can get away with it.

Although I am a few years away from getting some pussy, I have decided to bring up the topic anyways because there was a whole lot of praying and wishing for what I witnessed that night in my room. Since pussy plays such a big role in my life, from preteen to young adulthood to now, I feel the need to acknowledge pussy as being a power greater than I am.

THE FIRST BROAD
SHAKING MY HEAD (SMH)

I have been and will always be attracted to women. Moreover, I have always been damn selfish when it comes claiming one of them as mine.

I would write a girl the world-famous note asking the famous question, "I like you. Do you like me?" Then I would top it off with two options: yes or no. In my neighborhood, this was the way to pull a broad if you were seven years old or younger.

Shit started speeding up in the sixth grade. Mr. Fowler's class was off the chain! Kissing was the fad, and fucking was around the corner. When the rest of the class would leave, we'd stay behind to get a long kiss with some tongue. I'm not going to lie. I stayed behind only once the whole school year. I was not that popular, but all the girls just wanted to kiss me. Damn, I wanted to be popular! Something did happen at the end of the school year. To my delight, the popular guy was so popular that he no longer wanted who I wanted. So, he dumped her.

Well, you know what they say, "Another sixth grader's trash is another sixth grader's treasure."

It was a match made in heaven. This would be the best summer of my life. I would go to her house every day. We would watch TV together all day. We would sneak around and kiss all the time. We would walk to the free lunch together. In addition, after spending all day together, I would walk home and call her so we could finish the night out with a four-hour conversation over the phone about God knows what. Then sixth grade was over. We were on our way to junior high school, a bigger school with many more kids.

"No problem," I thought to myself.

On the first day of junior high, we did not even talk. Second day, same thing. Third day, eye contact! Yes! Nevertheless, there was no conversation. This went on the entire school year. I heard the rumors. My denial ran within me at an early age. She had been seeing another dude from my neighborhood the entire school year. He was light-skinned, had green eyes, was popular, and was athletic, while I was Black, skinny, and ugly with crooked teeth.

This feeling. It's showing its ugly head again. It is invading my peace and my spirit. I do not know what to do with it. Maybe I should sleep it away. On the other hand, maybe I should act as if it were no big deal. I need to do something. Life has turned on me once again, like in third grade! I am stuck. How do I maneuver through this? Maybe I will run. Better yet, go to sleep. I feel embarrassed, ashamed, angry, afraid, and betrayed. How can life be so fun and so beautiful one day, and then the next day, all hell break loose at the drop of a fucking dime? Life is showing two faces once again. I am getting tired of this shit.

SUMMARY

Although my self-esteem was on the floor and my ego was nonexistent, I managed to get through life turning against me for the second time in my short life. At this point in my life, I remember actually trying to make the connection between God and reality. I was actually reaching out to something—a power that was greater than I was—and asking it to restore me to sanity. And it did! However, there would be some permanent scarring.

Walking around feeling the way I was feeling was not healthy. I reiterate that insight based on hindsight is the fuel for this summary. Now that I am older, I can clearly see how this one episode played a major role in shaping who I was to become and my future relationships with the opposite sex. This caused:

- my inability to trust.
- my inability to be emotionally present.
- my propensity to control and manipulate girlfriends (physical abuse).
- my inability to commit to anyone or anything.
- my animosity toward light-skinned men.

What happened to me seemed like an ordinary child-hood breakup. But after searching and taking a fearless moral inventory, I discovered the long-term effects. One effect was my disgust for light-skinned Black men. I could never trust them. I could not stand to be around them. There was only a small amount of shit talking before my fists started flying. But the most damaging effect was thinking and believing that I was brought into this world and gift wrapped in darkness—my skin.

Also, all this shit happened before I could get my hands on some pussy. I was not even jerking off then. "LMFAO!" I needed a real break, and getting away sounded like a good idea. Going to 600 E. 27th Street was not even close to being far enough away for me. Not only did I feel very humiliated, but I also felt rejection, loneliness, fear, and uncertainty on top of my low self-esteem.

My thinking back then was like, "Lord, please get me the $%&* outta here."

Before I left, church would be forever instilled within me. Even when life turned on me with a bombshell, my coping skills were present. I was at the beginning of being resilient. Resilience is a precious asset. Without the ability to bounce back from letdowns throughout life, it could result in tragedy without a strong belief or support system. Nevertheless, what is up with life? Will it always be this bad?

On the other hand, should I ask, "Will it keep turning on me? Or will I ever be able to trust it?" How will I survive this two-faced jungle? More will be revealed.

CHAPTER FOUR

WHAT THE FUCK? (WTF) NOT AGAIN

ON AUGUST 8TH, 1981, I am on a side street at my grand-mother's house playing touch football with the neighborhood kids. A car drives by slowly. I cannot remember the model and make of the car, but I can remember who was driving. My good friend's mother was driving slowly, looking all sad with watery eyes. It took place within five minutes. However, at the moment, that shit took about three hours. She rode by, and our eyes met. And she did not even fucking stop. She spoke out of the car, "Michael Powell, your daddy just died…"

Life had bent me over again. Now I had to deal with some unfamiliar shit: death! Death of a close relative who wasn't really that close. My dad was my hero, even though his ass was never around. Picture that shit.

I can count on my fucking left hand how many times we were together. I remember he came to visit me at home, but my mother showed her ass and ruined that shit. She could've just stayed in her room with Ben and left us alone. Ben was the nigga that taught me a lot of shit like tying ties and shit. He was also the one stretching my hair and torturing the shit out of me once a year at picture time. Anyway, my dad didn't come to see her ass, right? Anyway, the visit was short. And to this day, I always wonder what if I was allowed to have that time, that moment, that precious conversation that should've, could've, and would've happened.

To this day, I still struggle to understand life and death. I don't care who dies as long as they are not my kin. I have lost people who were kin and with whom I had a close relationship with them. And I have lost people who were just close. None of it has ever been easy. When death comes to my circle of friends or family, I check mentally to see if I had been the best version of myself to them. I also have this need to know if I have taken them for granted.

My dad and I never really had a fair shake at building the typical father–son relationship like those on television. He left me at age eleven. I didn't know what a father was supposed to be like. I had one friend since I was five years old, and we were next-door neighbors for many years. His parents are still together to this day. So, I based my fantasy father on what my friend's father did for him. I know that men do have a powerful impact on raising their son into a man. I just know that I struggled without a father. If I had to choose which incident in life proved to be the most two-faced, it would be taking my daddy's life when I was playing tag football in the street instead of being by his side when he took his last breath.

CHAPTER FIVE

WHAT IF? IF ONLY. JUST ONE MORE TIME. ADDICTION.

WHAT IF I could do some shit over? *What if* I could go back to crucial moments in my life? I am talking about those life-changing moments. If only I could have done it right the first time around because life does not give out second chances. If only I would have trusted my mother's thinking instead of relying on my own immature, elementary thinking process. I have so many regrets that haunt my life.

So many times, I find myself saying, "Just one more chance. God, give me just one more chance." And guess what? I have gotten chances! But only in dreams and memories.

By the time I reached junior high school, fantasy was a big part of my survival skillset. Please allow me to explain. What if I actually could go back in time know-ing everything that I know now? I would be unstoppa-ble! I would be sucker-proof. That's right. I would be an eight-year-old with so much wisdom and knowledge that I would probably go fucking crazy. Prior to going crazy, what would I do?

Imagine waking up to being the smartest eight-year-old on the planet. Wait a minute! Since I know the fu-ture, it would make me the smartest person in the world. I would definitely, without a shadow of a doubt, fuck everything up. That's enough of the what-ifs. I just gave myself chills thinking about the mess I could make.

If I could play back some of those scenes in my life, I would do different things and say something differ-ent. Or I would say nothing at all. Who knows? The thing is, I would not be coming in last place in the goofy dude race. But knowing me and knowing the volatile relationship that I have with life, I would surely fuck something up.

I have some regrets. To be exact, I have four major regrets. And then I have several small, minor regrets that I have learned to live with and have pretty much forgot-ten about. The four that I will talk about have all been powerful lessons in my life that I live by today.

1. Doing wrong brings about Karma. There is no such thing as bad luck or good luck. However, I do believe in Karma, especially when it comes to life. This insight is based on hindsight. Whenever I did some dumb ass shit, I would usually experience some type of consequence. I was a decent football player, was really fast, and was on my way to play in college. I am 100 percent sure of this. But, for some reason, I chose to commit a crime against another human being. Nobody got hurt but me in the end. My two friends and I stole money and some weed from some guys who were out having fun and not bothering anyone. We split the money and used the drugs, and my dreams of playing sports at the collegiate level were crushed. Stories of Karma continued to follow me. This is just the first.

2. Stay put, dummy! Go back to the Navy, but it was not my choice. In fact, I gave it one hell of an effort to stay in. The Navy's SAM program was no longer in effect, and anyone who enlisted under this particular program would not be allowed to reenlist. Now this shit really

sucked! In my young and immature life, I had finally found some structure and security at the same time. But unfortunately, addiction found me first. And to be honest, I had a full-blown drug addiction before I even became a United States naval sailor. I actually overdosed before I was seventeen years old. The fun never stopped hurting. Today, I know without a doubt that having fun in the present can result in a lot of pain in the future, especially the type of shit that I was doing and calling it fun.

My discharge date was in early January. I had no direction, nowhere to go, and nothing to do. I was doomed at discharge and did not even know it. Based on hindsight, everything—and I mean everything—in my life was centered on getting and using drugs. And if I was not using, I was either in jail or finding ways and means to get more drugs.

In 1995, I had a God-given shot at reentering military service. But I still had a Satan-based addiction. This part of my existence was really the heart of the two-faced jungle. Life started whipping me regularly. Only moments of clarity popped up in short, well-dressed spurts. I could say to myself, "Everything is going to be alright." Then, bam!

I was set to reenlist. But I had picked up a felony charge. I had specific instructions to get the felony reduced. If I followed the simple, but difficult, instructions, I was back in. All I needed was $495. Now where in the fuck does a crackhead get that kind of money? It actually arrived in the mailbox in the form of an old government-issued check!

"Thank you, God!" I said aloud. But instead of paying off my fines so I could reenter the Navy, I smoked it up.

3. Go see your grandma! My grandmother was taking me to the bus station, and I was telling her that I was going to be back in about six months. She responded by saying, "I will not be here." When I returned, she was still here. Although she was hospitalized, she was still with us. I was partying hard. I was smoking crack, drinking, and fucking. In the midst of the frenzy, I called my grandma. We spoke briefly. I hung up with a promise to see her soon. Three

days later, after the party fizzled, I made my way to fulfill my promise to visit her. She had slipped into a coma the day before. I would never speak to the one woman who had always been there for me. I chose three days of pussy, crack, and alcohol over a priceless last conversation with my grandmother. This is a painful regret in my existence. I will never forgive myself.

4. Pulling out of the pussy. When I started getting pussy, it was coming in waves! I quickly became an international porn star in my own mind. All of the beating off in the bathroom at home in the middle of the night paid off. I knew positions before I was even fucking. And having a baby was a really big concern of mine. I knew that I could not afford a child. I knew that I was a child myself. So, what in the hell would I do with a child? This school of thought prevented me from ever impregnating a female while I was growing up. I was proud of this fact. I was boastful that I had no baby mama drama. Then I started realizing that I had held on to a way of thinking just a little too long. All of my associations had kids. My sister had four kids.

My cousins had kids. In addition, their kids had kids. I was childless.

I did, however, come damn close to having my own child though. In 1998, I messed around and caught me a young one who happened to live three houses up the street from me and my then girlfriend. It was the most stressful shit that I had ever been through at the time. I thought that I had gotten a woman pregnant while living with another woman. Until one day, the young woman's aunt drove out of nowhere while the older woman and I were out walking on a sunny day on February 14th.

She says, "Tell her or I will." Guess what? I told her what was going on with the young woman.

A whole two years dragged on. I was visiting the baby. I was really in no shape to have a baby. Nonetheless, the attachment between the me and child became real. Then, things got really different. We ended up in paternity court. Long story short, the DNA results were conclusive: it was 99.9 percent not mine. I remembered running to celebrate with the older woman. I also remember her not caring as well. My rationale was that at least she will not have a full-blown crackhead for a father. More will be revealed about the last statement in the next chapter.

BOOK TWO

ADDICTION: TRUE HORROR STORIES

CHAPTER 1
IN THE GRIPS: POOR ME

THIS CHAPTER IS where addiction really pulls his dick out! He "sho-nuff" lets me know who the boss is. They told me life was a good teacher. Guess what? I found this out. Throughout my young life, I came across instances where bad luck was sometimes to blame. Other times, it was the consequences of my own actions that brought about the pain and confusion. My first and only overdose happened on the night of June 25th, 1987, when I was sixteen. I didn't die. I woke up at seventeen.

Happy Birthday, Motherfucker

—The Devil

Addiction was not talked about in my early life because it was not a problem. Moreover, I really wanted the reader to see that addiction is much more than the amount or frequency a person uses drugs. I was told that addiction is the relationship with any mind-altering substance or experience that causes life-damaging consequences. Therefore, addiction was a part of my life long before drugs and alcohol took the main stage.

I was thirteen when the madness began. Just like everyone else who talked about when and how it started, I was having fun in the beginning. This is where my life slowly began to decline in quality. This is where those two-faced drugs were about to marry my consciousness. What I did not know was that I would be a slave for the next twenty years. Later, I realized that I was both the buyer and the seller.

When I arrived in Key West (with my eyes closed), I was a born-again Christian. I was uprooted from the comforts of home. The next thing I knew, I was in another world. All that bullshit about the *Wizard of Oz* was authentic. I tried tapping my heels together and thinking about home like Dorothy, but it didn't work! Not only was the Dorothy shit not working, but I also immediately dove into the same melodramatic thinking that this two-faced life has turned on me again. Poor little old me! It's time for some good luck to come my way. On the other hand, I thought…

My brother Darryl is dead now. I remember when we first began to interact with the island inhabitants. The first day, we were playing basketball with these white people. I got called a nigger for the first time by a little punk ass kid who did not realize that saying that to a Black person from North Carolina could get you fucked up. His older brother quickly stepped in to advocate, and my brother scolded me for going from being happy to "I'm going to fuck you up" mode.

Key West would later become the mecca of my knowledge as well as the beginning of the life experiences that would mold me into the person I am today. I've known that I am Black since the third grade. Key West introduced me to the concept of not having enough and not being good enough. The systematic part of racism revealed some of the harshest truths that I would ever have to accept. I was in the early stages of growing up. From the third grade to the eighth, I found out that life was really a two-faced jungle.

This is what I realized between the ages of seven and fourteen:

- I am Black. There was nothing that I could do about it. My only option is to make the best of a bad situation. Now I see being wrapped up in this black skin as a blessing today. This skin can be looked at as the coat of many colors that Joseph of the Bible's Book of Genesis wore.
- It's difficult growing up as a Black man. This turned out to be a plausible but incorrect statement due to a severe lack of information.
- Mixed relationships were forbidden to many people, especially Black people, with any other race. Newsflash: this turned out to be only a generational hiccup!
- I was poor. But ignorance really is bliss.
- I could use drugs and feel different. Every beginning has an end.
- Pussy was overrated. This will always be true! However, if every pussy on the planet dried up right now, pussies would still sell.

Looking back on my life between the ages of fourteen and thirty-two, I see I got in touch with how God, life, and the spiritual principles play an immovable part of my upbringing.

Addiction took me out not once or twice but several times. This condition—this state of mind—turned me against myself! I spent countless hours chasing a feeling that I would never feel again. Fourteen to thirty-two is eighteen years. Those eighteen years went by so fast. I missed every one of my benchmarks for maturity. My spiritual maturity was equal to that of a six-month-old infant. By the time I'd reached the age of thirty-two, I had missed life! I had been around the world with the military by the age of twenty-one. I was a full-blown crackhead by age twenty-three. By the time I was twenty-seven, I had almost lost my life twice, which didn't happen in the military. One was a hate crime in which I was the victim. The other was an attempted robbery in which I was the intended victim, but someone else got hurt. I had been in the penitentiary twice by the time I was thirty-two. I can't even remember how many times I visited the jail. I know that some visits were voluntary, depending on the weather. To this day, I still get chills thinking about how I believed in crack cocaine more than I believed in God.

BOOK THREE

RECOVERY

The Beast loves to eat black meat; it got us niggas
from the streets hanging of his teeth.

—Nas

ONE DAY, TRUTH and Lie went swimming. Lie jumped out of the pool, put on Truth's clothes, and started walking toward civilization. Although Truth had no clothes, it took off in pursuit of Lie. Truth eventually caught Lie and took its clothes back. This is the story of the butt naked truth catching up to the well-dressed lie.

March 23rd is the release date. I am at the crossroads once again. Something is different, and the difference is not on the outside. The world has not changed. This particular difference is on the inside of me! I want to take a stand against whatever force I have been up against for the past eighteen years. So far, this force has an undefeated record against me. Wait a minute. If I were asked about the worst relationship that I have ever been in during the last twenty years, I would have had a list of other people, places, and things to blame for my misery, pain, and difficulties in life. Today, however, I understand that the undefeated force that I thought was against me was *me*! *I* was the one who did not know how to say no to myself. *I* was the one who always wanted the easy way out. And when it came to obeying my conscience, that shit always went south. I was actually destroying myself one high at a time.

Step one: Once I think that I have control, I have already lost control. I always thought that when someone surrenders, they lose. But in recovery, I learned that when you surrender, you actually win. Understanding this paradox was so refreshing. A paradox is a statement that contradicts itself. So, by giving up and trusting God, I won my life back. I won my self-respect back. Then along came my dignity, happiness, health, and a host of other benefits that come with surrendering to win.

Being powerless is not a curse if I admit it and surrender. Surrendering means that I do less and allow God to do more. Although it's hard to accept the difficult things in life, I've learned that in order to heal from anything, acceptance is a pivotal step. Being able to admit and accept who I was and what I had become gave me peace and freedom. Surrendering is not about winning. Surrendering could be my ability to quit or give up (the bridge to step three). From this perspective, it becomes easier to do less and allow God to do more.

Even though I'll never be completely free of my uncontrollable desires, I have a high chance of never experiencing them on the same animalistic level as when I did in active addiction.

Step two: This is not a religious step that explains the great power of God. The main objective is to provoke thoughts and open the mind to things, people, and places that are placed in my life in many different forms from or through God.

I learned of one of the quainter definitions of insanity in 1996, when I was trying to get my shit together. Insanity is doing the same thing and expecting a different result. This understanding carried me for a huge chunk of my recovery because I practiced insanity for an even bigger chunk of my life. The second step opened my mind to different ways to look at situations in my life, and it gave me the ability to change directions while I was already locked in the preferred direction. In the beginning, this was a step with profound religious connotations. By having an open mind, I began seeing people, places, and things that had the power to change my mind, mood, and attitude.

Let's also remember the need for restoration. To be restored simply means that I was able to change my mind while heading down the wrong street. Feeling restored, however, is not a permanent feeling. You can feel the need to be restored once every hour, twice in an hour, or even multiple times at different locations before noon. The point is that this step does not promise to *do* anything permanent. Instead, it gives us a tool that will help us do something different instead of the same stuff when chaos and confusion show up.

Having previous experience with this step over the years, I know that definitions change according to the individual's program. That means an end to explaining, seeking approval, and explaining why I do what I do and how I do it. God knows, but he never intervenes. He always uses people, places, and things that he has placed in my life. People, places, and things do not make up who

I am, but they show me where I am. When shown my spiritual location, I am able to seek a way out. That is, if I want to leave.

Step three: I discovered another side to my rough-and-tumble life, and it was not pretty. The ugly side of life is and will always be ugly. I brought on the ugly side. This is the place in life where God was called on and people begged for his help—his saving grace. Deals were made with God here, and in the deals that I made, I believed that I would pay up, pay back, and pay attention. God would always show up. Sometimes he would appear as the police hauling my ass to jail or as treatment centers to get rest. What I understand today is that when he did show up, it was after I prayed for his help. I always promised to do better if… This is the place where the pain that I was in would always be self-inflicted. The way I live now and what I have are what I wanted. This was always God's will for me: to live and prosper. The evidence is undeniable. How I lived and treated myself showed that I wanted to die for one crack rock, one forty-ounce, or one set of consequences at a time. God has always taken better care of me than I have ever taken care of myself.

Thank God for the prayers that were prayed for me. God granted me grace and mercy. Grace means God giving me what I do not deserve (unmerited favor). And mercy is not giving what I deserve for my bad behavior. I know that prayer does not change his mind. Depending on how sincere the prayer is, it will determine how my mind will be reshaped to accept God's mind. I will no longer be able to get away with the fabricated, tailor-made version of God that I have been rolling with for all of these years. This God that I had come to understand was so flawed that he would be mad at whoever I was mad at. He understood when I had to resort back to old behaviors and actions. This God that I thought I understood was only available in emergencies.

Step four: I understood myself after I destroyed myself. And only in the process of fixing myself did I find out who I really truly was. —Sade Andreia Zabala

Step five: As I prepare to tell other people and God my story, I remember being scared as fuck. I am telling people things about myself that I am going to take to the grave, but these people are telling me that secrets would make you sick. Newsflash: I told someone, and now my secrets are exposed. Thank God for the fourth step. I can talk about the details in my story without having them be top secret. The truth hurts. This is not a war story where I am a superhero or something.

Step six: I realize that I have been walking around showing off new clothes while covering old wounds. This step made me aware that my problems went much deeper than the drugs that I used. Even though I was clean, I would still be going through the same bumps in the road that resembled my drug use. My thinking, my behavior, and my attitude kept me in trouble as if I were still using drugs. Recovery had to happen if I was to have any kind of freedom. The defects of my character would slowly creep in and take over the show.

Step seven: I am starting to understand that my God is tailor-made to fit my reality.

Step eight: I need to forget about what they did to me. Instead, I need to think about what I did to them! I have the opportunity to bring other people into my recovery. Not only do I bring them in, but I can also begin the reparations and forgiveness processes. I was an awful human being both while I was using drugs and while I wasn't using drugs. I must remember that this is not just a drug program. Even without the drugs, I still have those same shortcomings that were discussed in steps six and seven.

The list that I placed at the top acknowledges the harm that I have done to others. I know that I need to say "I am sorry." I understand that a true apology includes whatever I need to replace. I understand that saying hurtful things about something or about people is harmful. It is also what I failed to do for someone or something.

Step nine: If being doubly wrong with a conscience was a form of punishment, just kill me dead.

Step ten: After being clean and in recovery for nearly two decades now, I still find myself needing to adjust during the journey. The need to check my spiritual temperature still arises. Sometimes it occurs at inconvenient moments, and sometimes it is intentional. A lot goes on during the twenty-four hours that we call a day. The blessing of not being perfect produces circumstances that require study on my part. After a relatively speedy review, I've discovered that I am wrong. In fact, maybe someone else is involved. They are harmed and need immediate care. They have need and apologies. For this step to be effective, I will require the principles of self-honesty, integrity, compassion, and love. I am sure that there are many more spiritual principles that also apply to individuals who are in the recovery process. However, the ones that I named are applicable in one particular situation where this step proved priceless.

During a twelve-step meeting for recovery, I was rude to a new member and embarrassed him. I felt it in my gut immediately when I realized what had taken place. I knew that I had gone too far while seeking attention and praise for my groovy sharing. Unfortunately, it was at someone's expense. After I stepped out of the meeting to get some air, he followed and confronted me. I did not deny it. It felt like I was dripping with humility. By listening to him completely, I was able to empathize. He was pissed too. After he finished venting, he invited me to a brawl right there. But I opened up with a sincere affirmation that he was correct and that my behavior was unacceptable. After acknowledging my bad behavior, I apologized. We shook hands and hugged.

Step ten came to life in that moment. I checked myself and set the record straight because I was wrong. The second part of the step was even easier than the first. But if I worked on the first part with more diligence, the second part would not be necessary. Did I mention that the other guy stood about six feet and four inches tall?

Step eleven: Prayer is a presentation of my reflective thoughts and dreams to the only one who can bring them to fruition.

Step twelve: In the pursuit of perfection, I shall fail miserably in obtaining it. However, I will, along the way, spot Mister Improvement. I will run into Miss Excellence while chatting with my associate, Mister Good Job (a.k.a. Attaboy).

www.ingramcontent.com/pod-product-compliance
Lightning Source LLC
Chambersburg PA
CBHW031409160726
47993CB00003B/1162